Meditation

A Methodical Strategy For Reducing Stress, Improving One's Awareness Of Oneself, Sleeping More Soundly, Managing Pain, And Improving One's Memory

(The Absolute Necessity Of Meditation And Mindfulness, And How To Get Started With Both)

Edwin Paquin

TABLE OF CONTENT

Meditations Designed To Help You Fall In Love 1
The Reintegration Of The Asylum Seeker.........16
Moving Into Meditation - The Practice Itself...30
Guide To Meditation For Newcomers 43
Techniques Of Meditation Suitable For Beginners...50
Building Your Intuition Through Exercises 66
The Art Of Overcoming Obstacles While Meditating...77
Different Buddhist Meditation Practices...........80
While You Meditate, Take Pleasure In Being Fully Present In The Moment.................................87
Meditation With A Guide To Help Achieve A Sense Of Calm...95
Happiness Meditations Presented In A Guided Format.. 107
A Method That Doesn't Involve Meditating To Witness Your Thoughts 138

Meditations Designed To Help You Fall In Love

Meditation on Having Your Heart Open First

To get started, get yourself into a comfortable position. Take a seat, shut your eyes, and check to see that your back isn't arched too much or strained in any way.

Take a few slow, deep breaths and focus on relaxing the various muscles and tendons throughout your body. Wait until your energy has calmed down and you begin to have a sense of what's going on in the present.

Hold off on speaking until sentences come tumbling out of your heart. Give your heart permission to speak its most profound desires. Is there anything in particular that you've spent your whole life wishing for and dreaming of having?

Do you have any desires that you have never dared to act on because you were frightened of the consequences? Allow your heart to speak its desires out, even if you've been too hesitant to do so in the past.

"May I find love" is a prayer.

"May I discover joy in life"

May I have a carefree existence"

May experience contentment throughout their stay on earth"

Repeat your selected sentences in a slow and deliberate manner over and over again. Allow these sentences to calm your thoughts and take hold. It is very normal for your focus to stray every once in a while. If at any moment you get the feeling that you have already lost contact, you are free to let go and begin anew from the beginning.

"May I be loved, may I be happy, and may I have an easy life."

Make an effort to think of a person who has a special place in your heart. Someone who has never left your side, no matter what challenges you've faced. Someone who has inspired you in the past and who continues to motivate you to realize your full potential and live your life to the fullest. While you are seeing this someone, softly recite their name to yourself in the background. Make an effort to sense his presence and think of kind thoughts to send his way.

"May you always be loved and happy, and may life be easy for you."

Focus your attention on a person who has been going through a challenging experience during the previous several days. someone who has felt sorrow, wrath, disappointment, or grief at some time in their life. Someone who is currently dealing with a challenging circumstance. Imagine this individual is sitting in the chair directly opposite you. Say the person's name softly to yourself while simultaneously sending kind thoughts their way.

"May you always be loved and happy, and may life be easy for you."

Consider a person who plays a significant part in your day-to-day activities but whom you haven't had the opportunity to get to know very well. Someone who you would walk by without really noticing or recognizing their existence in the room with you.

Someone who you feel neither positive nor negative about. This individual may be someone you don't see very frequently, such as the cashier at the grocery store or the attendant at the gas station. Think warm and fuzzy thoughts about the person in question whenever you see them seated in front of you.

"May you always be loved and happy, and may life be easy for you."
When we use sentences like this, we are really inviting other people into our hearts. Instead of keeping some people outside of our sphere of loving compassion, we've decided to welcome them in. Instead of neglecting them, we are making an effort to engage with them. We are retraining our emotions to feel compassion rather than indifference toward others. Without making any kind of distinctions or setting any kind of boundaries, we are throwing open the

doors of our hearts to every living thing on every continent.

"May we be loved, may we be happy, and may we have an easy life."
our is for all people, animals, and all living things on our planet, no matter how close or far away they may be. regardless of whether it is known or unknown to us. Every living thing that exists on land, in the sea, and in the air. those who are now being born to those who are currently passing away. All living things that play a role in the cycle of existence.

"May we be loved, may we be happy, and may we have an easy life."
You may this moment feel this one-of-a-kind energy propagating outward from your core, all the way to the horizon. The energy is spreading in all directions, in front of you, behind you, and above and

below you. Both sides, front and back. It seems as if your heart is expanding in unfathomable and unanticipated ways that you could never have imagined.

"May all living things find love and happiness, and may they have an easy journey through life."
When you are ready, softly open your eyes, and allow this energy to continue to radiate from inside you as you go about your day. Have a heart that is full of expectation for the wonderful things that are yet to come.

Meditation for the Healing of the Heart

To begin, bring your attention to your breathing by taking long, calm breaths. Take a few calm breaths in, and then slowly exhale.
Bring your attention to the center of your chest. Imagine your heart

expanding as you take a deep breath in and out gently. As you let go of your breath, toss away all of the bad ideas that have been running through your head. Permit the opening of your heart, and then fill it with as much love and light as you possibly can think of. Imagine that your heart, which has been shattered, and all of its parts are being put back together again.

Allow yourself the opportunity to mend your broken heart at this period. Release the pain and errors of the past, and give the light that is filling your heart permission to heal the wounds it has caused. This illumination is going to make you more powerful right now. This light is what will help you reclaim your sense of yourself, which no one will ever be able to take away from you again.

Visualize this similar light traveling to any other parts of your body that are hurting, and the pain should begin to subside. Make it possible for the light to reach those regions and cure them. Imagine if your body and your heart are entirely healed.

Imagine that the love and light that is emanating from your heart is spreading out and penetrating every cell of your body as it makes its way outward. At this very moment, give yourself permission to be overcome by a sense of calm that will permeate your whole existence.

During this activity, you can experience a rapid onslaught of feelings, both positive and negative. You simply need to recognize that it's the way things are and open your heart to the experience. When you notice that you are beginning to feel overwhelmed, put yourself in the position of an observer and give yourself permission to experience whatever is going through your head. Allow it to come to the surface, then begin working to get rid of it.

Take several deep, steady breaths in and out until you feel like your emotions have diminished. Imagine that your whole body is being bathed in love and light and that it is entirely being restored. This is your opportunity for a new beginning, a new life, and a new you. Give yourself permission to be excited about the new possibilities that will soon be presented to you.

As you begin to accept your new reality, it might be helpful to keep the following affirmations in mind.

"Right now, I am on the mend. To be healthy in body, mind, and soul"

"I am no longer held captive by the past. My life is now free of all the suffering and errors that it has produced.

"I am making progress in restoring my health. I am becoming better at appreciating the fact that my health and welfare are the foundation upon which my life is built.

"Let go of the past and seize the opportunities that lie before you in the here and now. The future that I've always envisioned for myself is now within my grasp.

"I am being made whole by the transformative power of love and light. I am thankful for the chance to become well that this presents.

As you come out of this meditation, see the light closing up your heart and restoring it to its regular functioning condition.

When you are ready, slowly open your eyes and bring yourself back into the present moment by focusing on your breathing.

You may better establish your footing on the ground by taking the seated stance. After you have finished with that phase, you will need to direct your attention to elongating your spine in such a way that it both raises you up and enables you to keep your equilibrium for the duration of the meditation session. In order to properly carry out this practice, your spine must be as straight as an arrow.

Having said that, it is difficult to totally extend your spine and hold it 100% erect right from the beginning of the exercise. Maintaining the straightest back possible will make it much easier for you to become used to the routine. If you want to keep your back straight, you should make an effort not to slouch and instead spread your shoulders.

If, on the other hand, sitting upright in a normal position causes you to experience discomfort or agony of any kind, you should try sitting with a support behind your back or even lying down. It will take time and effort for your spine to extend to its full potential, so try not to be too harsh on yourself right now.

The third point of posture is to relax and rest your hands.

Your hands should be the next primary area of concentration for you. It is in everyone's best interest to let them relax on your lap. Nevertheless, you might hold them on your side or rest them on your thighs as an alternative. It is claimed that by placing your hands palm down on your lap or thighs, you may encourage energy to flow more freely throughout your whole body. When you keep your hands on the ground, you are allowing the energy that is flowing through you to migrate out of your body and into the floor, which disturbs the energy flow that is occurring inside your body. Keep your hands on your lap or in any other position where they are resting on your body to prevent this from occurring.

You may also rest your hands in your lap at the level of your navel while placing your right hand on top of your left hand with your thumbs barely touching one another and letting your hands rest in this position. Because it generates a sufficient amount of heat and energy in your body, this position keeps you attentive throughout the practice.

4. Unwind Your Shoulders This Is the Fourth Point of Posture

The next thing you need to do to relax your shoulders is to softly roll them backward. This assists in establishing a strong, lean back and opens up your body at the same time. Additionally, it frees up your heart and makes it possible for energy to enter your body without obstruction.

In this context, it is also essential to discuss the fundamental make-up of your hand and the ways in which it facilitates communication between you, your mind, and the rest of your body.

The Reintegration Of The Asylum Seeker

When we deviate from what God has called us to do, we will experience consequences. You can't toy with evil and put yourself in harm's way and then expect to be unaffected by it. When you play with fire, you open yourself up to certain risks. Dorian Gray's image in Oscar Wilde's The Picture of Dorian Gray is so tainted by the deterioration caused by his depraved and hedonistic lifestyle that he feels the need to conceal it and keep it hidden away. When Dorian finally has a chance to look at the image after all these years, he is shocked to realize that he does not recognize his own face. Sin has such repercussions for its victims. The more time we spend engaging with the world and its practices, the greater the impact the world's tiredness will have on our own selves. For this reason, we need to keep our hearts and thoughts guarded in the Lord Jesus Christ. The apostle encourages us to direct our attention toward the heavens. Think about these things, putting into practice what we have learned and been given, and whatever is true, whatever is honorable, whatever is just, whatever is pure, whatever is lovely, whatever is commendable, if there is any excellence, if there is anything worthy of praise, think about these things. If there is anything worthy of praise, think about it. (Philippians 4:1-9) Those verses. While gazing at the splendor of the Lord, we are all being changed into the same image as we go from one level of splendour to the next. (18 of the Book of Corinthians).

THE FOURTH CHAPTER
A MYSTICAL SCIENCE THAT IS KRIYA YOGA

Kriya yoga is a wonderful scientific practice that has a remarkable spiritual potential.Mysticism is defined here. Mysticism may be understood as a field of study in which the focus of one's attention is directed inside, with the goal of gaining insight into some fundamental reality. These inner forces are very potent and tremendous in scope.

Why should one turn inwards?

The inner world is a vast and formidable realm that has a tremendous deal of power and potential. This powerful force has a tremendous deal of potential and power inside each of us. Humanity will never be able to fully grasp these concepts because they are just too complicated. Because our minds are so focused on the world around us, the vast majority of our energy is constantly directed toward the outside world. This flow of energy in a more external way occurs via our senses. The goal of spirituality is to redirect these outwardly focused energy to become more inwardly focused.

This complicated idea has to be broken down and investigated using scientific methods. The first refers to a person's mental state, while the second refers to their level of awareness. The states of consciousness include waking, dreaming, and sleeping respectively. The state of mind is comprised of one's thoughts, feelings, and memories of the past. The many states of thought may be compared as waves crashing against the shore of the ocean of awareness. In order to broaden our awareness, we need to still the waves of thought that are occurring inside us. Therefore, bringing the mind to a state of calm is very important in order to enable the pure awareness to emerge. our pristine awareness is what makes up the fundamental forces at work in our cosmos.This widened awareness is a force that has a lot of potential and strength.

To have a grasp on this idea, we first need to comprehend the several layers that make up our existence. The vast majority of us constantly exist in two different worlds: the exterior world of our senses and the interior world of our ideas. The most fundamental aspect of our life is right here. Imagination and seeing something happening is a more potent kind of force than thinking. The visualization process has a greater potential for success than the materialization one. The first indication that our minds are growing is when we start to practice controlled visualization. The majority of the time, our imaginations and the ability to visualize are a tremendous instrument of mysticism that we possess.

Our minds are an incredible resource that can help us grow. The goal of practicing Kriya Yoga is to broaden our own inner energies so that we may grow in a way that is multifaceted.

MEDITATION USING THE HITBODEDUT

The rabbis of the middle ages kept hitbodedut meditation a closely guarded secret.

Ancient Kabbalists have been engaged in this particular kind of meditation for many years. In modern times, it has been streamlined and transformed into private prayer and communal meditation; nevertheless, we must take care not to confuse and mix up the many different types of meditation.

In the first iteration of the Hitbodedut meditation, the kabbalist would sit outside among the trees and strive to transcend material existence without really leaving his body. Instead, he would try to transcend material existence by separating himself from the material world and becoming closer to the divine.

This meditation is distinct from the Devekut meditation in that, during the Devekut meditation, the adept maintains control of the meditation through the use of reflective expressions and key words, whereas in the Hitbodedut meditation, the kabbalist makes contact with the divine while attempting to leave the physical consciousness and enter enlightenment while making contact with the divine. When a person reaches this point, all gross physical stuff ceases to exist, and they enter a spiral of light that leads them closer to the divine.

How can a meditator with no prior experience start practicing this more sophisticated kind of the practice? The first thing you need to do is seek for locations in nature that are associated with Kabbalists. Your spirit will travel and make touch with the One Who Created Everything while you are outside in nature.

When you become in touch with the divine via the practice of common meditation in nature, Hitbodedut will occur spontaneously, linking soul awareness to bodily consciousness. As a result of this, the material world will no longer have a purpose, and you will be able to experience the divine in all of its splendor and grandeur.

This method ought to be second nature, much like riding a bicycle. When this occurs, you should stop practicing traditional meditation and instead allow the spiral of light take control by establishing a direct connection with the divine.

It is something that originates from deep within, not from the human mind itself but rather from the manifestation of the Holy Spirit (Ruach Kadosh).

You can really connect with your spirit if you meditate outside among the trees. In due time, every earthly worry will yield to the illumination of the divine.

This is not a simple task; yet, writing, speaking, or practicing a common form of meditation is simple, and the instructions for doing so can be found in the literature; but, developing a relationship with the divine is something that takes time.

It is possible to find relief via the practice of transcendent meditation. During this technique, you pretend that you are in a holy place or in nature, even if you are sitting in your own home. This allows you to detach your mind from the material world, as well as the restricted conscious mind that is related to your regular existence. This may be a method to go to Hitbodedut, but the simplest approach is to meditate on nature. To do this, you should seek for a mountain, a deserted beach, a water source (whether it be a river, lake, or sea), and do your best to let go of the anxieties that attach themselves to your everyday activities. Because our soul, the NEFESH, can quickly detect nature and effortlessly interact with the natural world around it, this is much simpler to do in natural settings.

This meditation is very similar to the Indian practice of Samadhi, which is considered a very profound kind of meditation in which the meditator transcends the realm of physical matter and integrates with the divine and the supernatural.

In Hitbodedut, you get to comprehend that the divine is superior to you and that there is no need for you to beg for anything since everything is already under the care of the divine. You also come to realize that in due time, his blessing, all that he promised, and everything you desire will reach you.

When you get to this point, you realize that it is pointless to pray the same petition a thousand times, since he is in charge of everything, and the response will arrive at the proper moment for it to be received.

Hitbodedut is also prayer, but rather than praying with the bodily conscience, one prays with the conscience of the soul, seeking to discern the will of God not just on their own lives but on the lives of all people and all of creation.

We were a part of the process, which is something that is hard for people from the West to grasp since we are so focused on what we want for ourselves and so little on what comes after us.

We will make a giant leap toward the light when we meditate and pray for others, especially for the sick world, and when we do so, Rabbi Yeshua's words will come true: "If you are in me and my words are in you, you will ask the Father for everything you want in my name, and he will give it to you."

This is something that no one in the West can comprehend; the person in question may believe that he is only inquiring, but in reality, he is missing the bigger picture, which is that everything is a part of the process of the Eternal kingdom shining in this corrupt world so that eventually, good will triumph and darkness will be driven away.

As long as our egos continue to blind us to this reality, we will continue to find ourselves in the same predicament, much like the boatman who was attempting to row against the stream. The teachings of Hitbodedut instruct man to completely submerge oneself in the process in order to comprehend the divine mystery.

This method ought to be second nature, much like riding a bicycle. When this occurs, you should stop practicing traditional meditation and instead allow the spiral of light take control by establishing a direct connection with the divine.

It is something that originates from deep within, not from the human mind itself but rather from the manifestation of the Holy Spirit (Ruach Kadosh).

The Hitbodedut meditation also has a more profound significance and a more spiritual component. In this particular instance, the variable at issue is not nature but rather our current condition of being. When we are confronted with an intractable situation that has an effect on our soul and there is no way out of this Hitbodedut process, the state of being that we are in is the fact that we meditate, so establishing ourselves in the divine light and putting all pain and problems to the side.

Because this world is transient and a deception, because this world is a fraud, only the light of the Creator counts, fix your soul in the light during the time of deepest anguish because this world is a fraud.

Keep your focus on the light inside, the light that is so pure that it cannot be corrupted by evil.

The concerns are insignificant in comparison to the holiness of this light.

This meditation on getting away from difficulties is not really an escape at all; rather, it is an encounter with the universe of 99% while running away from the restricted world of 1%.

while Jacob fled away from his country, he did so because he was scared of his brother Esau. However, while he rested by a rock, he forgot about his anguish and agony and entered a condition of light known as the state of Hitbodedut. It was at this time that he saw the stairway of angels, on which angels climbed and descended.

The light that he saw and felt was larger than his issues, and to merge with the divine is to become Hitbodedut, which is what he saw and felt.

Problems and suffering are both illusions; the reality is found in meditation; it is in the light that penetrates our spirit with such force that we are rendered speechless and all agony is removed.

Moving Into Meditation - The Practice Itself

When you enter a meditative state, it indicates that you are shifting from one mental and physical state to another as you move through the practice. Imagine you are going through a doorway or a gate. This is the point at which everything will get underway. Before you can pass beyond that threshold, you have to first find a comfortable seat, loosen your muscles, breathe deeply in and out, and bring your mind and body to a state of serenity. After you have finished all of those things, you should start visualizing yourself over the boundary. Now, give this topic of meditation (crossing the threshold) some thought and see if you can bring it into your consciousness.

What are some other topics that you may meditate on?

Symbols and Visual Representations

Having the ability to think in images is not only a helpful talent but also makes visual meditation a lot less difficult. The majority of individuals prefer the notion of meditating or thinking with symbols and images since it helps them develop and bring things to mind. These prompt more in-depth contemplation of more abstract notions and ideals such as love, depth, knowledge, and the passage of time. Some people find that seeing what they need to do helps them recall stuff, organize ideas in their heads, and even put up a timetable.

Thinking using traditional symbols is an effective way to communicate concepts about religion, society, and the afterlife. Consider a candle that has been lit as an illustration. The meanings of hope and tranquility are instantly sent to the person who sits quietly and focuses on a candle that is lit. Some people focus their meditation on moving bodies of water, such as lakes and rivers, which are symbols of ongoing life. Some on rose windows, which are symbolic of the entry of light into several churches.

Taking into consideration the natural world The majority of individuals think that meditating on natural elements, such as waterfalls, the sensation of sand on their feet, the sound of the waves, and even trees and mountains, is very calming. The many symbols that originate from nature are all included in the language that is understood by everyone. Recurring patterns may be seen across the landscape thanks to the natural world. It is analogous to a mountain, which symbolizes fortitude and tenacity; the sun, which stands for a source of life; and waterfalls, which stand for power and creativity, among other things.

Step 2: Delve even farther into your meditation.

As you cross the barrier into step 1, you start your journey into meditation. This is the beginning of your practice. You may see yourself walking through an open door. Now, how about we delve even further? Imagine going through the door to see what's on the other side. You might begin to see a large home with a number of rooms and entrances in it. Imagine that as you continue to go deeper, you are entering door after door, and then all of a sudden you see a stairway and choose to descend it.

A word of advice: try not to hurry things. It is quite OK for you to go slowly but steadily. When you try to picture the scenario in your head, be sure to engage all of your senses. The instant you go through one door, then another door, and then proceed down a flight of stairs, it denotes that you are delving more deeply into your own psyche.

When you have reached the bottom of the staircase, do not rush to climb it just yet; there is still some time until you may do so. You could start exploring, or you could search for a quiet place where you could simply sit down, settle down, and relax. After you have developed this "inner world" via the practice of meditation, you may take use of this skill to enter a deeper level of meditation.

Meditation helps you become more in tune with all of your senses, which may free your creative side. You will become more awake and aware of everything that is going on in your everyday life if you meditate regularly. Fostering one's creative potential may be accomplished through strengthening one's visualization abilities and cultivating one's imagination. As part of the process of becoming more fully yourself, discovering your own unique form of creative expression is essential. Your ability to constructively cope with the many problems that life throws at you will improve if you do so. Keeping an active imagination helps keep your mind sharp, allowing you to get the most out of every session.

Allow your mind's eye to become open. As you go further into meditation, it is essential that you allow your mind's eye to become open. What strategy do you plan to use to accomplish this? You make an effort to not only describe the recollections in words, but also to do it via vision. As you think, you can even conjure up detailed visuals in your head. To put this to the test, let's speak the word "water" and see how many different things it brings to mind. Imagine a river or stream with water flowing through it. Now, let the water flow in your hands as you see it doing so in your mind. visualize how satisfying it would be to relieve your thirst as you visualize the water flowing over your skin, how clear it is, and how it feels.

What are some of the other ideas that spring to mind when you think of water? You have to understand that the more you utilize your creative imagination, the more real it will seem to you. Your ability to meditate effectively utilizing "imagery" will improve if you regularly practice using your "mind's eye." During meditation, you will be asked to generate images in your mind's eye. To get the most out of this exercise, let your imagination go wild. You will have the opportunity to use your ideas without any restrictions thanks to this. What strategy do you plan to use to accomplish this? Imagine you are carrying a box that is empty. When you toss this box into the air, the box vanishes from your line of sight. When you look at it, it seems to have bunnies jumping about on it. Keep an eye on them as they jump about you. You extend your hand to grab a rabbit, but it suddenly transforms into a ball before evading your grasp. When you examine the ball in further detail, you will see that an image of a rabbit has been carved inside of it. This is one way in which you might use your creative faculties. It ought to have no boundaries.

What should I do if I find it difficult to concentrate because I am easily distracted? There is no need for alarm. This is to be expected. As you get further into meditation, a large variety of mental distractions will present themselves to you. It is as if you suddenly find that your thoughts are drifting aimlessly and without any prior notice. If you see this happening, do not continue down this path; rather, gently pull yourself back into meditation or into the topic you have chosen to focus on while practicing visualization. At first, it can seem like a bit of a challenge, but eventually, you'll get the feel of it.

In the same manner, if you have trouble seeing something, you might attempt to conjure up a picture in your mind by drawing on all five of your senses. Do not restrict your attention just to the sense of sight or touch. Use all of your senses to their full potential. Because your memory is so rich with memories, it is impossible for you to not have at least one in which you may fully immerse yourself.

Do you remember the smell of the pine trees or the sound of the waves? Experiment with different combinations of the five senses to see which one gives you the greatest confidence.

Look at some of these instances to see what I mean:

The more of your senses you engage, the more potent and vivid the sensations you have on the inside will be.

Therefore, do not be scared to test your limits and get familiar with your skills. Who knows, maybe you'll find another ability or talent you never knew you had.

Your sense of touch: when you shut your eyes, can you remember what it's like to run your fingers over the fluffy fur of a dog?

Do you have a strong sense of smell? Can you remember the smell of a newborn from memory?

Sense of taste: Are you able to differentiate between various flavors in your head?

Do you have a sense of sound? If you close your eyes and use your imagination, do you think you can hear the sound of an instrument being played?

Sense of sight: Are you able to remember as many different events as you possibly can?

The third step is to come out of meditation.

When you have done with your topic, have explored utilizing your imagination, and have arrived at the level of inner peace and tranquility that you were striving for, it is now time to let go of your focus, dissolve the mental images that are now present in your mind, and gradually emerge from the meditative state that you were in. After having crossed the threshold mentally entering the internal world, it is now time to mentally exit the internal world and return to the world outside the threshold. Do not be in a hurry. When you are ready, slowly bring yourself out of the meditative state. Give your body the opportunity to resume its usual breathing pattern. Take your time when you shift your attention to the farthest parts of the planet.

The fourth step is to get ready to rest.

Take some time before going to bed to sit still and think about what happened throughout the day. Consider the events in question as if you were viewing a movie in your head. Attempt to take note of your personal involvement and think back to the events that took place on that day. Try not to focus too much on the things that are going wrong. Do not try to remember the full experience if it was a horrible day and you had a lot of challenges on that particular day. What is the purpose of include this in your meditation practice? Through engaging in this practice, you will be able to cultivate a sense of perspective and continuity that will strengthen every facet of your life. This sort of reflection on one's day is helpful, particularly in situations in which it might be challenging to juggle a variety of duties, obligations, and responsibilities, as well as competing demands from work and the family.

When you attempt to recollect the day without criticizing yourself or the other people in it before you go to sleep, you are turning your thoughts and focusing on yourself instead of other people.

Guide To Meditation For Newcomers

Meditation might first seem overwhelming or impossible to beginners. This is OK. This is quite normal, and things will only get better from here. Meditation is a skill that has to be practiced. After all, it is quite the undertaking. It is vital that you continue to practice and perfect the technique of meditation in order to reap the benefits, therefore it goes without saying that you should keep on keeping on.

When you are anxious, it might be challenging to focus on a single topic for an extended period of time, which is necessary for the practice of meditation. You are going to want to begin your practice of meditation with concentration meditation since it is the most straightforward of the several kinds of meditation. Finding the concentration necessary for effective meditation may be accomplished by concentrating on a single mantra and your breathing at the same time. You may focus your attention on anything in the immediate environment, such as the wick of a candle or the tip of a pen; the choice is entirely up to you. As soon as you start concentrating on the thing that you have chosen, you will stop paying attention to the other things that are going through your head and instead give your whole attention to the thing that you are concentrating on. Even while it isn't always simple, if you put in the effort to perfect this talent via practice, there is nothing in this world that will make you feel more at ease.

Finding a spot in your house that is both comfortable and spotless is essential for meditation. When individuals meditate, they often sit on the floor and cross their legs; however, if this is not feasible, they may always use a chair or a meditation cushion instead of sitting on the floor. In any case, it is a wise decision to have a meditation cushion within easy reach for whenever you may need it.

When you want to meditate, you need to make sure that you have had enough of rest. In order to get the most out of your session, you need to make sure that your mind is as fresh and awake as it possibly can be. Before beginning your meditation session, check to make sure that you have not taken any form of medicine or ingested any alcohol.

Before beginning to practice meditation, make sure that you have had enough rest and that your stomach is not too full. This is just as essential as making sure that you are well-rested. It is much more difficult to meditate while one's stomach is full, therefore whenever it is feasible, make sure that you have not ingested any form of food for at least two hours before to your meditation session. Meditating on an empty stomach is preferable whenever it is possible.

You are now prepared to get started! Make sure that you begin by dressing in something that is comfortable. If you can help it, steer clear of jeans. While you are meditating, you should take off your shoes since there is a significant likelihood that you will desire to do so. If you'd rather wear socks, that's also OK.

Reduce the brightness of the lights in the room. If you want to utilize candles for your meditation, now is the moment to light them up. In addition, you may bring things that make you happy into the space where you meditate, such as flowers, incense, and other such things.

Now, keeping your back straight, sit down on the floor (or chair, if you've decided to use a chair) wherever you feel most comfortable. If you are sitting on a chair, propping yourself up using pillows and cushions is a totally acceptable method of doing so. You should now remain motionless in the posture that you have selected and start concentrating on your breathing as soon as you can. When you find that your thoughts have wandered away from the activity at hand, bring your attention back to the act of breathing. You should take calm breaths in and out, and you should keep thinking about those breaths so that you may become aware of how you feel when you inhale and exhale. You may choose to close your eyes if you prefer. Always keep your attention fixed on the breath that you are taking and center your thoughts on that single inhale and exhale. After a few minutes of sitting in your quiet potion, you should feel as if your mind has disconnected from the outside world and the rest of your thoughts. Keep your attention completely on the act of breathing, concentrating on each individual breath.

You might also concentrate on a single mantra (which could be a word or an item) and repeat it again and over until you are able to focus your attention completely on that phrase or thing. Again, if you find that your mind is wandering and thinking about other things, you should just pause, bring your attention back to your mantra, and then begin meditating once again.

Beginners often find this to be the most challenging aspect of the practice. If you find that you are unable to concentrate as much as you would want to, try not to be too harsh on yourself about it. Conquering this requires a significant amount of work, and the more practice you put in, the simpler it will become for you to do.

This is a meditation session, and this is how it should be done. It is so simple, but intricate all at the same time. When you have achieved a level of mastery in meditation and are able to empty your mind completely, you will question why you did not begin practicing meditation earlier.

Techniques Of Meditation Suitable For Beginners

If you are just getting started with meditation, it is recommended that you begin with mindfulness meditation. Meditation on present experiences, often known as mindfulness meditation, is one of the most popular and accessible types of meditation.

To begin meditating, it is important to recall the stages that were covered in the first chapter. When you meditate, you should make sure that you are neither too full nor undernourished. In addition to this, check that you are well hydrated and that you are dressed in loose, comfortable clothing.

The Most Fundamental Mindfulness Exercise - Take a seat on a chair or a cushion if you want. Take several slow, deep breaths and bring your attention to your breathing. Maintain awareness and focus on your breathing. If your mind starts to wander and you find yourself thinking about things such as your job, the food you consume, the people you are in relationships with, or anything else, bring it back to your breathing. Don't pass judgment on yourself. Simply become aware of the idea, release your attachment to it, and direct your attention back to the breath.

A Technique of Mindfulness That Will Help You Become More Aware of, and Heighten, Your Sensations Throughout Your Body – Sitting in a chair and taking slow, deep breaths is a kind of mindfulness meditation that may be practiced in a number of different ways. Take note of all the feelings you are experiencing right now in this very now. Take note of the prickling sensation that you experience in your toes or the tension that you feel in your fingers.

Spend some time focusing on the feelings that are occurring throughout your whole body, from your head to your toes. Take note of everything that can be heard, seen, smelled, and tasted. You may label them, but you shouldn't pass judgment on them. Perform this activity every day for at least five minutes. Mindfulness may initially present some difficulties for you, but if you master the skills necessary to train your mind, it will become as natural to you as breathing.

The Heart of the Rose Meditation Technique is a fundamental kind of concentration meditation that was used by Buddhists of the past. You may use any flower, however a rose is recommended for this exercise. Take several slow, deep breaths while seated in a chair that's comfortable for you. Take a good look at the rose's core, often known as its heart. Place the majority of your focus on the flower, and pay close attention to its shape, color, and texture. If you find that your thoughts are wandering, try to identify what you are thinking and bring your attention back to the flower. You may practice this kind of meditation for a total of five minutes each day for the first week, after which you can extend your daily meditation session to ten minutes. This method will assist you in taming and mastering control of your thoughts. This method will assist you in being more present in the here and now as well as more attentive of your thoughts and behaviors. You will find that it is much simpler for you to replace negative ideas with positive ones on a day-to-day basis if you use this strategy.

It is recommended that you set an alarm so that you will not be required to check your watch at random intervals. It is also a wonderful experience to meditate beside a mentor or a loved one. It will be much simpler for you to keep your promise to yourself to meditate on a regular basis if you do it this manner.

Caused by an Uneven State in the Sixth Chakra

One of the most prominent signs that our sixth Chakra is out of alignment is the presence of fear. Living based on fear changes our reality by implanting beliefs, illusions, and feelings that do not exist; it merely causes that afraid to make any choice or route, we get paralyzed and do not act in a constructive manner, or even worse, we don't act at all!

Dependence on substances like drugs and alcohol warps our perception of reality, taking us to places that are not as they seem and putting our lives in jeopardy. This leads to the formation of false and terrifying illusions that have the potential to put an end to any existence and any aspiration to transcend. Guilt is another component of the imbalance; it is often forced on us by the ancient religious dogmas that restricted both our acts and our ideas by portraying man as a creature without bravery in the eyes of God. Guilt is a factor in the imbalance. Accepting pain as a kind of self-punishment for being "sinners" is the root cause of human misery, which can be traced back to this point.

Another sign of imbalance is when we lose sight of things and, rather of integrating as part of a whole within the Earth or the Universe, we "self-situate ourselves" as superior creatures. This occurs when we believe that, because we meditate, do yoga, or pray, we are on a higher spiritual plane than individuals who do not lose touch with reality. The belief that we shall gain entrance into paradise if we are willing to face the agony and the sorrow associated with "being good" is another example of an extreme that is the outcome of a separation. We are all connected in some way, and while our individual paths may diverge from one another, we are all moving in the same direction—that of development.

One of the ways that we might become aware that there is an imbalance in our lives, even if we do not want to notice it, is if there is any kind of hardship, discomfort, or pain in any facet of our lives. Pain and suffering, whether they be physical or spiritual, are signs that something in our lives is not functioning as it should, that we are headed in the wrong direction, and that we have something to improve upon. If we speed up the learning process, we will also speed up evolution.

Keeping the Check and Balance

The harmony that results from establishing a connection with the natural flow of life energy is ideal. At this juncture, it seems that you have arrived at the appropriate location at the appropriate time. When you do this, you begin to connect with the wonder that is life, and miracles become a natural part of your experience. Without actively seeking them out, opportunities and events will present themselves to you. Even if you believe yourself to be nothing more than a bystander to life, other people may see you as a "star" person, a visionary, or a prophet.

You have acquired the ability to live in an environment characterized by peace and tranquillity, free from conflict, and in an ongoing state of happiness. You are in the midst of a world rife with evil and bloodshed, yet no one touches you. You tend to attract others who share your nature.

There will be moments when you feel disoriented and as like you have "lost the ground." When you are in a situation like this, you should search for the voice of your subconscious to help you meet your path and the light. Some of the available possibilities include the practice of meditation and yoga. In addition, you might seek for books that provide you with new motivations for your life, books that contribute to your knowledge, philosophical notions, and a new period of life; writers of Masters and Spiritual Guides are some examples of these types of authors. There are further methods to "get the voice out" of our subconscious; divinatory arts such as tarot reading and rune casting may help direct you in the right direction.

You might use the following practice of guided imagery as a supplement to maintain the sixth Chakra: The consolidation of everything that is.

The Meaning Behind the Sixth Chakra of the Soul

You may be of assistance to other people by demonstrating another way of living to them when you have developed the ability to perceive and experience a reality that goes beyond the mundane, one that is vast and transcendent. People may be shocked by the ease with which things are provided to you as well as the strength of vision that you possess; this will cause it to approach you, learn from your knowledge, and you would like to open up new avenues in your life.

Sahasrara, the seventh of the chakras
Violet is the color.

Crystals, including Transparent Quartz
La Coronilla is the location.

The seventh Chakra, which is positioned in the crown, represents the whole confluence of energy. This Chakra represents the unification of our own experiences with those of the larger community. The whole essence of deity itself is contained inside it. Once we have activated this Chakra, everything divine is presented to us in every instant of our existence. At this level, we are no longer content with just knowing about God; rather, we want to integrate with him and experience it. When we first arrived, we saw people through human eyes, but now we see them through the eyes of god. We get an understanding of his very being. When we look at every occurrence through the lens of spirituality, we realize that we are, in essence, experiencing the miracle every day.

When we reach this point in our development, we begin to engage in strange behaviors since our conscience has completely shifted. The spiritual guides who are given to the spirit are a part of this group. Keeping this consciousness of divinity is not a simple task since any trace of fear would bring us back down to our lower chakras. If the six chakras below it are not in proper alignment, we will be unable to activate the seventh chakra. Because it is the one that encompasses everything, this Chakra is the one that is the most difficult to master, as it requires the other chakras to be in perfect harmony for it to be activated. This is the ultimate goal that our soul has set for itself.

The choice of whether or not to embrace the responsibility that this degree of knowledge brings to us is what will keep us at that level. When we decide to live through our seventh Chakra, we are embracing the obligation that this level of information brings to us. If we choose not to receive it, we will be sent back to the lower chakras; but, if we do choose to accept it, the unending energy of the divine will be with us as we work toward the attainment of the goal that our soul has set for itself.

People around us will be drawn by our energy and want to be with us because the tranquility we inspire, the learning opportunities we provide, and the fact that we are able to represent an example and a guide will make them want to be with us. When you live through the spiritual, you prefer to live alone, pondering nature and your spirit.

Being at this level allows us to accomplish extremely well since we are able to grant people's wishes by drawing on the divine energy that is available to us. This happens naturally because there will also be a taste in you to help other people, and we will be provided with a special divine connection, as well as their energy. Because of this, it is essential that we maintain the connection with the divine, as well as balance, because when we are out of balance, people will continue asking us for help, and in that case, we will continue giving it, but not through the divine energy, but rather through our own energy, which will end up exhausting ourselves.

The discord that exists inside the seventh chakra

At this point, the presence of an imbalance is quite hazardous.

Because we are experiencing totally spiritual experiences, we are able to cease having a connection with everything that is mundane. As a result, we no longer have a relationship with other people or with respect to the material world, and we see both of these things as having a lesser amount of significance.

Fears are an additional risk factor since they may materialize into potentially dangerous things. It would not be as significant at any other time in our lives since fear does not manifest itself, but in this circumstance, we will be seeing and perceiving creatures who have the potential to disrupt our psychological tranquillity and urge us to take them to a mental health facility if the situation becomes too severe.

Another imbalance is the "whim of asking," which occurs when we integrate the knowledge of the new age or metaphysical teachings. These tell us that compiling a list of what we need and asking for it as if it were already part of our reality is the best way to attract what we want into our lives. It's possible that this will make everything manifest, but at the same time, this list is being produced by our ego, and we have a tendency to believe that our ego knows more than God does. In this situation, it is preferable to resign to God since He is the one who knows the most about us and what we need, much more than we know for ourselves.

Building Your Intuition Through Exercises

In order to successfully complete this task, you will first need to assess your feelings and then assign a color to each of those feelings. You might employ the conventional meanings ascribed to different colors, such as red signifying anger and blue indicating healing energy. However, in order to get the most out of this activity, you should choose a color scheme that speaks to you the most.

To get started with this exercise, think about a circumstance that is simple, like exchanging a text message with a person who may become a possible companion or lover. It's possible that you're thinking either loving or hateful thoughts about this individual. Love may be represented by the color pink or red, while contempt could be represented by a darker hue like black or purple. The color you choose to represent your sentiments of love or disdain should depend on how you personally feel about this circumstance. Keep in mind that there is no such thing as the incorrect choice of color, and that you should choose the hue that you personally would connect with your emotions.

You will start to rewire your energy such that you identify this hue with this specific feeling as you continue to engage with this person and this emotion in the future. You will be able to enhance your intuition by associating colors with this activity, and you will be able to interact with your intuition in a nonverbal way through these colors that are based on emotions. Your intuition will eventually get more in touch with these color schemes, and it will be able to signal to you via colors so that you can perceive the wider picture of a situation. This will take some time.

If you have previously associated the color red with love, for instance, and your friend is talking about a particular person, and you are able to see the color red while she is talking about them, then you will intuitively know that there is a loving connection between the two without your friend having to express this directly to you. This is because you have previously associated love with the color red.

The process of scanning a room in order to gain a sense of the atmosphere of the location in which you are practicing is another technique. This is done when you are positioned in the middle of a room that does not include any other individuals at the time. You have the option of moving around the energy of the place by moving your eyes in order to see what is going on, or you may physically travel around the room to see what is happening. Make sure to keep track in your head of the smells, sounds, and images that you are taking in. Ask yourself where you are being drawn to energetically and if there are persons or locations that you feel you should steer clear of. Be as specific as you possibly can by scrutinizing the furnishings, windows, and corners of this area, as well as how your interior state is affected by these features.

The more you engage in this activity, the more prepared you will be to carry it out in a setting that contains a number of other individuals. This is a more strenuous form of the exercise, and depending on how sensitive you are, it may be difficult for you to complete it the very first time. Pay attention to your body and stop if you feel like it's reaching its limit. You should not, however, allow these nervous sensations to distract you from the process of improving your talents. Along the journey, there are going to be growing pains and testing, but after you push through these experiences, there are going to be amazing rewards waiting for you on the other side.

You may do this practice in a variety of settings, including public transportation, workplaces, pubs, and parks. You will be able to continue to strengthen your connection with your intuition and get more acquainted with the energies of your surroundings if you are able to use this approach in locations that you visit on a regular basis and in which you have access.

Utilizing your subconscious and the dreams that you remember is yet another activity that you may perform. It is via your dreams that you are able to digest and absorb the energies that you come into touch with during the day that have not been especially resolved. This is because your dreams are your subconscious mind's way of communicating with your conscious mind. Because it is impossible for us to maintain a healthy and balanced living if we take in every experience that we have in a single day, our psyches come into play to assist us in finding the kind of equilibrium that is necessary for a life that is both functional and healthy.

You are able to free yourself from the restrictions of this physical plane by engaging in dream work, at which point you will be able to roam about easily in all kinds of settings and on other levels. It is not uncommon to run with spirits from other worlds, to go into the past as well as the future, or to visit regions that are not your own. Because there are no boundaries to the areas that may be explored in the subconscious, there is a never-ending supply of hidden potentialities to unearth there.

Keep a notebook and a pen next to your bed so that you may jot down any insights that come to you during your sleep and make the most of the information that your subconscious mind imparts to you. In the real world, it is all too typical for you to forget the experiences you had and the knowledge you gained in the dream world. You may combat this propensity by making it a routine to jot down whatever it is that comes to mind as soon as you open your eyes in the morning. In this manner, the information will be fresh in your memory. Even if you can only recall a fragment of your dream, it is important to write it down. While you are writing down the one element of your dream that you recalled when you woke up, you could discover that you are able to remember other parts of your dreams as well.

This is a routine that should be done every day, and it may also be done at any time throughout the day. Developing your intuition demands you to be conscious of the company you keep. Pay attention to the individuals you hang out with. Make certain that the individuals who are a part of your inner circle are trustworthy and that they have a good frame of mind. If at all possible, cut away the people in your life that are a drain on your energy. Take note of how much more intuitive you feel when you are in the presence of particular individuals. If you see that it gets better while you're engaging with them, you should try to spend as much time as you can with them. Staying away from individuals who sap your energy is the best approach to preserve the potency of your intuition, particularly while you are still in the process of honing your gift.

Asking your close friends about particular pieces of advice and information that you are getting is a great way to put your intuitive talents to the test and see how accurate they are.

When your sentiments and sensitivity are validated by your intuitive abilities, you'll be better able to put your faith in them and use them to guide your decisions. As you cultivate a stronger faith in your intuitive abilities, you will become better able to depend on them, and as a result, they will get stronger.

You will be better prepared to take on the difficulties of strengthening your intuitive talents now that you have the foundation to assist you with your daily self-care procedures. Let's look at some different methods that you might improve upon your existing skills and capabilities.

The cumulative impact of stress on one's professional and personal life over time

The impact of stress on both your personal and professional lives may be dangerous, in addition to the negative effects it has on your health. Let's take a look at the risks that are associated with this endeavor.

You are someone who may easily get "burned out." Being exhausted from your job is the last thing you want to happen. That will almost surely guarantee that your productivity will go completely out the window, as the expression goes. In addition, while you are working at such a frenetic pace, you will discover that even when you are not exhausted, your productivity will be nowhere near as high as it should be. This is the case even if you are not exhausted. On top of that, you eventually begin to feel as if going to work each day is a "chore" when you get up in the morning. You realize that you have virtually no control over the events that may be going place in your life, and by the time the day is finished, you are completely worn out. It's possible that you could even find yourself wishing that you had a clone of yourself who could help you do the task faster so that you wouldn't be so behind schedule. Overall, it seems as if you do not look forward to coming to work and instead go about it in a rather mechanical manner, without any pep in your step.

Your connections with loved ones, including friends and family, become strained. If you work too much, your relationships with the people who are closest to you and most important to you will definitely suffer considerably. Because of this, being in your company is no longer a delight, and you may even discover that others are moving away from you at a faster rate than you are from them. You become grumpy and irritated, and you would much rather stay in your room than attend to parties where everyone is 'happy' except for you, of course. You would rather to remain pent up in your room. This type of imbalance between work and life leaves no time for the vital small things that count in life, like being able to attend your son's baseball game or your daughter's ballet recital. This has the potential to make you more irritable, which may then lead to repressed rage, which can negatively impact your job.

There is a chance that you won't keep your job or be promoted. These hazardously high levels of stress may have a detrimental affect on your work to the point where you could be passed over for that promotion that you have been working so hard to get, and perhaps you might even wind up losing your job as a result of it. This has the potential to completely upend your life, and not only will it be too late to make any changes to the existing scenario, but it also has the potential to make your mental state much worse. When in reality, it had the potential to be held in check a very long time ago already.

The Art Of Overcoming Obstacles While Meditating

Both of these chapters have focused on instructing you on how to meditate properly. They may be a little too much information to comprehend, and a lot of it doesn't make much sense until you really get started with the whole procedure. When you first start meditating, you may find it difficult to believe that something as fundamental as breathing could be so beneficial; nevertheless, you will soon discover that there is more to this than meets the eye.

HOW TO SEARCH FOR A JOB

When I first began meditating, I had a lot of problems that needed to be solved. The first one was a real pain in the neck. I began my practice of meditation by sitting, but I quickly discovered that it was difficult for me to remain seated on the floor. It was difficult for me to stay in one posture for an extended period of time, which often resulted in discomfort and stiffness. My trouble was that I had first had a very fixed conception of what meditation entailed. I was determined to carry out all of the tasks in the prescribed manner. However, I quickly came to the realization that there could not possibly be firm laws about something as malleable as meditation. You must rather make it your own by customizing it to meet your requirements in order to do so. Therefore, you should meditate for as long as you feel is necessary and in whatever posture seems most comfortable to you.

RANDOM IDEAS AND THOUGHTS

This issue was simple to solve, but the next one proved to be much more challenging. My mind was constantly going in a million different directions, and my emotions were all over the place. I had heard that having mind wander is one of the most prevalent problems, but that it becomes easier as you develop your ability to concentrate on anything. The important thing is not to give up; rather, you should strive to concentrate on each breath, taking it one at a time.

Different Buddhist Meditation Practices

Vipassana and Samatha are the two fundamental approaches of meditation used in Buddhism. Although they serve distinct purposes, they complement one another in the process of strengthening the mind of the practitioner, which ultimately enables that practitioner to attain the ninth awareness.

Samatha is a kind of meditation.

The concept of "Samatha" is comparable to what we mean when we use the words "tranquility" or "concentration." The majority of us have brains that are always busy with a stream of different thoughts. It is not feasible to investigate higher levels of awareness unless we have first mastered the ability to still our racing thoughts and improve our capacity for focused attention. Samatha meditation is practiced in order to get these benefits. The practice of Samatha meditation is one that requires very little in the way of preparation. It entails concentrating on a particular subject without allowing the attention to stray to other things.

Breaking the negative patterns of behavior that we have cultivated over the years is the most challenging aspect of meditation for the majority of individuals. The majority of us have lost the capacity to concentrate on ourselves because we have been trained to pay attention to the world around us. In addition, we are always looking for something new and exciting, which is particularly true in today's world and one of the primary reasons why mobile phones have become such an integral part of our everyday lives. Our mobile phones, with their capabilities of emailing, text messaging, and accessing the internet, satisfy both our need for unique experiences and our need to be stimulated. When we meditate using the Samatha technique, we are getting to know a deeper part of ourselves, a part that may provide us with total satisfaction without the need for a binding agreement.

When a practitioner is able to concentrate their whole attention on a single target, the practitioner's mind will eventually become still, and they will feel a sensation of ecstasy. This rapture is the outcome of focussed attention, which in normal circumstances is fragmented due to the activity of ideas.

Meditation via Vipassana

Vipassana meditation is a kind of deep meditation that may be used by the practitioner after they have developed the capacity to bring their mind to a state of serenity and concentrate their attention on a particular object. Vipassana meditation is different from Samatha meditation in that rather than concentrating on an object, you focus your attention on yourself. The focus that was created via samatha meditation becomes the instrument that is used to eliminate the layers of illusions that hinder us from instinctively understanding the ninth consciousness, which is our enlightened nature. This is accomplished by removing the layers of illusions that lie between us and our enlightened nature.

In light of the fact that humans are unable to directly experience the ninth awareness, I have purposefully settled on the phrase "intuitively knowing" to describe it. The ninth awareness is one that cannot be sensed or felt in any way. It is neither a picture nor a feeling that we have. The tenth conscious is our actual essence, yet it is not something that can be experienced in the physical world. You may be wondering how I'm expected to acknowledge it if it can't really be experienced. The solution is straightforward. You can determine what you are not by working backwards from the situation and eliminating possibilities. When you eliminate all that it is not possible for you to be, you are left with nothing. The only way to get at this revelation, which can only be gained via firsthand exposure to it, is for you to come to the conclusion that the truth about who you are.

Vipassana is a practice that has to be done on a consistent basis in order for one to find their actual selves, and the amount of time it takes until one comes to this revelation varies from person to person. The euphoria that is experienced during Samatha meditation is only felt for a short period of time, but the understanding of one's own nature is something that can never be lost.

The practitioner of Vipassana meditation develops the ability to be fully aware of their thoughts, feelings, and emotions without being involved with any of these aspects of themselves. They are also aware of the transience of all that may be experienced in this life. Our ideas, perceptions, and feelings are continuously forming, dissipating, and shifting in intensity in response to our environment. The practitioner comes to realize, and this is perhaps the most essential benefit, that he or she is not their mental processes. Your ideas, perceptions, experiences, or anything else that you may be experiencing are not the same thing as who you are.

Vipassana and Samatha are the two primary types of meditation practiced in Buddhism; however, there are many additional types of meditation, and many of these meditations incorporate aspects that are also present in other types of meditation. It is beneficial to categorize meditations according to the following four distinct styles: concentrative, generative, receptive, and reflective. This is because there are many various types of contemplative activities. You will find exercises to practice in the next chapter, so that you may become proficient in all of these activities.

While You Meditate, Take Pleasure In Being Fully Present In The Moment.

In addition to the traditional form of sitting meditation, there are a variety of alternative methods and approaches that, when added to your meditation routine, may assist you in calming your mind and just being present in the moment. The following are some suggestions that might help you learn to still your thoughts and focus on the here and now.

1. Get in the habit of walking meditation. Walking meditation is a kind of mindfulness meditation that combines movement with the practice. When you practice walking meditation, you concentrate on your breath and your steps, taking a few moments here and there to take in and take pleasure in the scenery around you. Meditation while walking is a particularly efficient practice for quieting the mental clutter and anxieties that might cloud one's

thoughts. It teaches you to be present in the here and now.

2. Develop a close relationship with your ideas and communicate with them - The majority of us just let our thoughts to pass through our heads without paying any attention to them at all. As a direct consequence of this, your mind is always racing with anxious and negative ideas. Take conscious note of your ideas. Create space in your schedule every day to sit quietly, concentrate on your breathing, and put into practice some of the fundamental mindfulness methods that we covered in the chapters that came before this one. Whenever a thought crosses your mind, just acknowledge it without passing judgment on it, and then return your attention back to the breath.

3. Give Your Mind a Break - Whether you're at work or in class, make sure you give your mind a break at least once a day. Take some time to clear your head, relax, and rest your mind. During your

lunch break, give yourself some time to just sit at your desk and do nothing, or take a stroll around the neighborhood for a few minutes.

4. Don't think about anything at all One of the most sophisticated techniques for calming the mind is to force oneself to think about nothing at all. This indicates that one must suppress an idea in order to prevent it from entering the mind. It also implies that you should constantly edit your ideas in order to avoid being controlled by your thoughts. People who have developed great mental power through the consistent practice of meditation are the only ones who are capable of using this method.

Do not go through life acting as though you are merely going through the motions. Try not to live in the past or let your worries about the future consume you. The only way to really appreciate the present is to train your thoughts to be still.

Joy and pleasure

Living in the present and appreciating the experience of being alive are essential components of happiness. That is the level of simplicity it can reach. There are two easy approaches that you may do if you believe that you might benefit from some assistance from meditation in order to have a more positive outlook on life.

Contentment in the Here and Now

You may use this extremely simple method of meditation whenever you feel the need to improve how you are feeling in your life. Savoring the little joys that life has to offer is all that is required.

The first thing you need to do is choose one easy and delightful activity that you often do not enjoy to the same degree as you would otherwise. A few instances of this would include preparing a meal, going for a stroll in the park, sipping a steaming cup of coffee, luxuriating in a warm bubble bath, or spending time with your pet.

The next thing you need to do is allow yourself to take pleasure in this action and let your senses soak up the good vibes. Be conscious of the good emotions that accompany the action, such as relaxation, joy, and love. These are the sentiments you should focus on.

That sums it up well. To experience joy in one's life might not need any effort at all. Perform this activity on a daily basis for about one week, and then, at the conclusion of the week, pay attention to how you feel in general as a result of the experience. Do you have a greater sense of calm and positivity as a result of it?

being in a state of contentment

Think on everything that went on throughout the day before going to bed. When you thought about it, did you focus more on the positive or the negative? Have you been focusing more on your victories or your defeats? The fact of the matter is that you have the ability to exert some control over your own thinking. People who are successful and happy make a conscious effort to enjoy life to the fullest. When they do experience failure, though, they see it as a separate incident rather than as something that gets ingrained in who they are.

You might use the following meditation practice to assist in the development of this attitude inside yourself:

Take some time to relax and breathe deeply while seated in comfort. Recall all of the joyful experiences that have occurred in the last twenty-four hours while you continue to breathe normally. It might be a tender moment shared with a close friend or a member of one's own family. It may be something as simple as a wonderful dinner, as moving as a short film, or as fun as a minute spent romping about with your dog. Relive the whole event in your mind and savor the sensation of happiness it gives you while you do so.

Feelings of satisfaction and appreciation should rise up from the depths of your being in response to the amazing things that have happened to you in your life. If you have trouble recognizing these emotions, try putting your attention on your heart and opening yourself up to the feelings that are triggered when you are shown love and concern by other people.

You may continue to build on these feelings by thinking back on all of the joyful experiences you've had throughout your life. Remember to maintain a steady, deep breathing pattern.

Imagine those unpleasant recollections passing past like clouds whenever they pop into your head. Keep only the pleasant recollections in your mind. Revel in all of these pleasant recollections for as long as your heart desires.

You should do this easy workout just before you go to bed for the best results. It has an almost immediate effect of making you feel cheerful, and it also helps ease pain and exhaustion, allowing you to enjoy a better night's sleep as a result.

Meditation With A Guide To Help Achieve A Sense Of Calm.

This exercise is meant to help you calm your mind and reduce the rate at which your thoughts go through your head in order to make your life more serene and harmonious. It is recommended that you meditate on a daily basis in order to get the optimum outcomes.

Find a spot where there is peace and quiet. Get into a posture in which you are most at ease, whether that be sitting or laying down. To improve your breathing, realign your spine. Take your time to breathe (around 20 seconds).

Put your hands somewhere to relax them totally, and then continue. Inhale, then exhale for a total of twenty seconds. You should close your eyes and loosen the muscles in your neck and shoulders. Take a moment to breathe deeply (around 20 seconds). Imagine that a load has been taken off of your shoulders. Inhale and exhale for a total of twenty seconds.

From this point forward, focus on your breathing and let go of any stray ideas that come into your head; this is the automatic exit mode. You should give yourself permission to relax, feel the lightness moving through your whole body at the time of your breath, feel your lungs filling with air, feel the life entering your body via the breath, and concentrate your attention on this for a few minutes (around 20 seconds).

Take a long, deep breath in and then gently let it out. Take some long, slow breaths. Give your body twenty seconds to relax and adjust to the pattern of your breathing before beginning. While you are going through this process, love yourself. Raise your awareness to your body, concentrate on all of its activities, and come to the realization that you are the marvel that life is.

Listen carefully to every sound, both coming from inside and coming from outside the surroundings. These noises are not meant to distract you; rather, they represent an indication of what is going on in your immediate environment (20 seconds). Continue taking slow, deep breaths and focusing on relaxing your body. Continue to inhale for ten seconds, or until you become aware that your lungs are completely filled.

Exhale, then let out your whole breath after ten seconds. Maintain your attention on the breath you're taking. If you find yourself having distracting thoughts, try to let them go for the next twenty seconds and concentrate on your breathing instead. Take a few deep breaths.

Relax and let the air out slowly. Let rid of whatever assumptions you have for any topic for ten seconds. Your sole responsibility is to concentrate on your breathing, pay attention to the flow of life in harmony, and maintain a calm state.

Take a deep breath in and hold it for twenty seconds before gently releasing it. Let go of every judgment you have, both about yourself and about other people.

Let go of any and all expectations. Maintain your concentration on the tranquility of the present while simulating a deep level of relaxation for the next ten seconds. When a new thought enters your mind, direct your focus back to the flow of your breathing, and then let the idea to go back to where it originated.

Feel the air entering your body as you inhale, and then as you gently exhale, feel the air exiting your body after a count of twenty seconds. You have twenty seconds to let yourself relax and focus on being present in this moment. Become aware of the rhythm of your heartbeat, and take note of how calm it feels. Take a minute and a half to breathe deeply three times. Give yourself permission to carry that sense of serenity with you throughout the day.

SIXTH CHAPTER

Consuming Food Consciously
This one might be challenging due to the fact that eating has become a kind of

emotional support for a lot of individuals. And there are instances when we are completely oblivious to the fact that we are doing it. I've had bouts of mindless eating throughout my whole life, and until very recently, my weight was like a rollercoaster, always going up and down. Recently, I've been able to break free of this cycle and am finally at a healthy weight.

The issue is that most of the time we don't give much thought to the foods we consume or the reasons behind our decisions. Sometimes, in an attempt to satisfy our feelings, we eat even when we aren't hungry at all; sometimes, as a kind of self-punishment, we deny ourselves enough food to eat; and occasionally, we only provide ourselves with bad food alternatives, and then we wonder why we feel exhausted and unhappy.

By practicing mindful eating, you may steer clear of all the latest fad diets and stop your weight from fluctuating erratically. You will get the awareness necessary to make healthy decisions about the food you consume and the quantity of it when you practice mindfulness. It's about recognizing the extent to which we're preoccupied with instant satisfaction and working toward a state in which we treat ourselves more kindly.

One of the most important aspects of mindful eating, which was made famous by the mindfulness movement, is taking your time and genuinely savoring the flavors of the food you consume. This is essential, without a doubt, but it is also about treating oneself with compassion. We need to bring ourselves to a position where we are comfortable in the concept that we deserve a pattern of eating that will nourishe us, make us feel well and happy, and not lead us down a route that will be detrimental to our health in the long run. Consuming unhealthy foods may provide you with a satisfying flavor in the moment, but it is not very nice to yourself in the long run. Instead of berating ourselves about how we've performed in the past (even if that performance was just five minutes ago), it is essential for us to adopt a more forgiving mindset and go to work improving our awareness of the world around us. We have no choice but to proceed, just as we do whenever a distracting idea enters our minds during meditation.

Reader, it's possible that you're already at a point in your life where you eat completely healthily and are doing an outstanding job in this aspect of your life. That is just amazing! However, you may still benefit from these strategies in your practice of mindfulness due to the fact that each meal is a new chance to be aware that is built into your calendar.

The following is a list of the most important aspects of practicing mindful eating:

1. Reduce your speed. Give yourself enough time to enjoy the flavor of your meal by taking a moment to savor each bite while you chew it. Think on the fact that you're doing something positive for yourself (assuming you're eating something nutritious, that is!). Even if it's something that isn't great for you, at

least take your time eating it so you can taste it and take in all of the different flavors and sensations. Take the time to savor what you're eating. When we shovel down our meal and then feel like we need to eat again right away because we believe we are not satisfied, eating more slowly enables us to reach at that moment of fullness at a better speed than when we shovel down our food and then feel like we need to eat again because we are not satiated.

2. Do not eat if you are not in the mood to do so. This should come as no surprise, yet a significant portion of the food we consume is not for the purpose of providing our bodies with fuel. We want to be able to pick at something while watching a movie; we want to be able to blend in with everyone else at a party that includes a dish of food; and we believe that eating a pint of ice cream would in some way make us feel better when we are upset or angry.

3. Make an effort to steer clear of distractions, such as watching television or glancing at your phone. This does not

mean that you have to abstain from those items indefinitely, but I highly recommend that you do so as you become used to this new way of eating and awareness in general when you make the transition. Demonstrate to yourself that you are capable of doing it. When we are paying little to no attention to our food because we are watching television or reading an article on our phones as we eat, this indicates that we are not really enjoying our food.

4. Be aware of when you eat due to your emotions. At first, this may involve nothing more than becoming conscious of the errors in your decision-making. This is a step in the right direction toward getting some distance between your emotions and the decision to overeat or make a food choice that isn't the best for you. There are times when we need to be exposed to an unhealthy routine several times before we finally decide to put our foot (or fork) down and make a change. Practice having patience with yourself.

5. Give more attention to how much alcohol you consume each week. It is common knowledge that drinking alcohol in moderation is not only safe but also acceptable, and there are certain individuals who are able to do so without difficulty. Perhaps one or two glasses of red wine, savored slowly so as to take in all of its nuances of taste. However, we also know (most of us from personal experience) that alcohol lowers inhibitions, and I can personally confirm that in my situation, regardless of how well-intentioned I am about drinking thoughtfully, I find that I am in a horrible position after only one drink. This is the case even if I try to drink mindfully. Almost immediately, I have the want to nibble on anything, and if I'm already eating at the moment, I always consume more food than I require at that point in time. It's not a big deal if you do it once in a while, but it becomes problematic if you make it a habit. When you do decide to indulge, pay attention to your routines and make an effort to drink in a

conscious manner, taking care to do so slowly and deliberately.

6. Determine which foods are your triggers. What kinds of meals put you in the mood to gorge yourself? It is really difficult for me to control my eating when I am surrounded by crackers, chips, and cheese. Once I get started with some items, I almost immediately begin to regret my decision, but I keep eating anyhow because I have the impression that the harm has already been done. I believe this is what occurs. How ridiculous. However, we do not need to fully abstain from meals that cause us to lose our minds; rather, we need exercise caution around these kinds of foods. These are the kind of meals that need our utmost attention and caution. Would you want some ice cream? Do not bring the pint into the living room to watch late-night television with you. Put a couple of scoops of the ice cream into a bowl, and then sit down at a countertop to eat it. If you're really craving it, that is. Consume it and focus on appreciating the flavor. When you give anything a

more thoughtful taste test, you can discover that it does not have quite the same allure as you remembered it having. (Okay, this is probably not going to be something you find out with ice cream, but if you take the time to be interested about the tastes, you may find that other items you typically consume may not taste as good as you used to believe they do.) When we eat in this manner, it may allow us the space to recognize whether we are making bad choices while they are still occurring, and gradually, we will be cognizant of this before reaching for that food like a zombie again.

It is something you do on a regular basis, without fail, so it gives you with constant chances to exercise your mindfulness and establish a daily routine. Mindful eating is fantastic in a similar way that mindful bathing is great: it is something that helps us become better eaters, and it is also excellent in a similar way that mindful showering is great.

Happiness Meditations Presented In A Guided Format

I. Meditation with a Focus on Experiencing Joy

Turn down the lights, and choose a secluded spot where you may relax in peace.

Create a comfortable environment for yourself while also relaxing your muscles and putting yourself in a calm condition.

Place your hands on your lap, and shut your eyes as gently as you can.

First, take a few deep breaths, and then just relax.

Allow yourself to make a connection with your inner being while keeping your eyes closed. Get completely absorbed in your own ideas and emotions. You will eventually become more conscious of your surroundings as the world around you begins to recede into the background.

Take advantage of this state of relaxation and prepare both your mind and heart for what is ahead. Allow yourself a few minutes to relax and get your thoughts organized.

Put all of your worries to one side for the time being since you are now free from all of your obligations. You won't be affected by your issues here; this place is a refuge of peace.

During meditation, if you find that your thoughts have wandered, you should simply return your attention back to your breathing. Take some deep breaths, settle down, and find solace in the calm that is inside you.

Remind yourself that you are the one in charge of the situation. You may return to your own world at any time by doing nothing more than opening your eyes.

Inhale and exhale slowly and deeply. Take a deep breath in and then out. Take a deep breath in and then out. Take a deep breath in and then out.

You have a greater sense of calm presently. You are completely unconcerned about anything in the world.

Once again, be sure to take calm, deep breaths. Take a deep breath in and then out. Take a deep breath in and then out. Take a deep breath in and then out.

Right now, you have a sense of serenity and tranquility. Imagine the best possible outcomes.

Once again, be sure to take calm, deep breaths. Take a deep breath in and then out. Take a deep breath in and then out. Take a deep breath in and then out.

It seems as if you are drawing ever-nearer to the state of ecstasy with each breath that you take.

When you imagine happy thoughts, you may physically feel your heart growing larger in your chest.

You are now prepared to go on this guided trip to your own inner joy, a haven of peace that you can claim as your very own.

Permit yourself to conjure up images that make you pleased. Don't try to push things. As you take long, steady breaths, give yourself permission to let things happen naturally.

Free yourself from your inhibitions and set aside your expectations. Give your imagination permission to conjure up whatever pictures it pleases.

If the visuals aren't coming to you readily, you might try visualizing your perfect environment via your senses instead. How does the air make you feel when it touches your skin? What type of aroma do you pick up on here? Do you hear anything at all? Permit yourself to get completely immersed in the event.

Imagine that you are perched atop a hill, and that in front of you is an open green field.

Imagine that the sun is warming your face and the rest of your body.

Imagine the tickling sensation of the grass on the tender flesh of your bare feet.

Imagine that you are far away and you hear bird sounds. Try to picture the soothing sound of a nearby babbling stream.

Imagine being at ease in this setting for a moment. Imagine you had an infinite amount of time to take in the beauty of your surroundings without any interruptions.

Imagine for a moment that you are protected in this building that you call home.

Imagine being completely happy and fulfilled, with no desire or need for anything else in the world.

Please allow yourself some time to sit back and take in the breathtaking views and tranquil atmosphere. Walk around and get a feel for the different areas.

You will experience an even deeper sense of relaxation and tranquility as you make your way around this mental paradise.

Picture a large tree with wide leaves growing close to where you are right now. Take baby steps in the direction of the tree until you arrive at your destination below it.

Take note that the tree is laden with delicious fruits in a variety of sizes and forms that are dangling from it. This unique tree produces fruit that, when consumed, will bestow upon you a variety of distinct supernatural abilities.

Extend your hand and pluck a fruit from the branch that is resting on the ground. Examine the piece of fruit that you now have in your grasp for a bit. Feel the touch of it and the weight of it in your palm in addition to just looking at the color of it.

Take a bite out of the fruit and allow it to satiate both your physical and mental hunger.

As you continue to chew and swallow the fruit, you will become aware of an increasing warmth throughout your body. The feeling will start in your upper chest and go to your heart, followed by spreading to your arms and legs.

Foster this sensation of love and joy that you're experiencing in your body. Put an end to your thoughts and concentrate on the sensation instead. You will experience a light that is otherworldly and a feeling of happiness that will spread through your whole body.

Take another taste of your fruit, but this time focus on savoring each and every mouthful you take. Allow the feeling to get stronger as the flavor develops.

When you take a third mouthful, you will notice that it radically alters the way you see the world. You are experiencing a level of joy that is unmatched by anything else in the world right now. Permit the warmth that is contained inside you to emerge and permeate the world around you.

Take in the serene atmosphere and savor this time set aside for reflection on your own happiness.

You may decide how long you wish to spend meditating.

Simply opening your eyes is all that is required to bring your meditation to a close when you are ready. Before going back to your regular schedule, you should give yourself a few minutes to relax and get used to being awake before getting back to work.

Meditation on Life's Little Pleasures

Put the outside world behind you and set out on a path to discover the pleasure that is inside you. Find a spot where you may quiet your thoughts, unwind your body, and become one with the calm that resides inside you.

Turn your attention to your breath while you close your eyes.

First, take a deep breath in, then let it out.

First, take a deep breath in, then let it out.

First, take a deep breath in, then let it out.

Imagine that you are on a beach with sand and that the sky is clear and the sun is shining. You look up to see the sun just rising, and a refreshing wind is blowing in your face.

You have a peaceful disposition, a sense of comfort, and contentment with your existence.

You are standing carefree on a beach all to yourself, oblivious to the outside world. You have a plenty of opportunities to spend time alone with your emotions and ideas.

You have a peaceful disposition, a sense of comfort, and contentment with your existence.

The sound of waves lazily crashing into the coast is what you are now listening to. You decide to stroll towards the ocean, and as you do so, you become aware of the sensation of chilly water under your feet.

You have a peaceful disposition, a sense of comfort, and contentment with your existence.

Imagine for a moment that you are standing on a grassy hill in the middle of the day. You are about to see one of the most breathtaking sunsets ever as the sun begins to drop behind the hills.

You have a peaceful disposition, a sense of comfort, and contentment with your existence.

You are standing on the ground close to the woods, and without having any unfavorable thoughts in your head. You have a plenty of opportunities to spend time alone with your emotions and ideas.

You have a peaceful disposition, a sense of comfort, and contentment with your existence.

You are in the countryside, and you can just make out the sound of birds singing. You begin out in the direction of the setting sun, and as you walk, you feel the cool grass under your feet.

You have a peaceful disposition, a sense of comfort, and contentment with your existence.

Now picture yourself on top of a hill, looking out at the star-filled night sky below you. The moon is shining brightly, and you can make out a myriad of twinkling stars in the sky above you.

You have a peaceful disposition, a sense of comfort, and contentment with your existence.

You are completely at ease while being in the most precarious position imaginable. You have a plenty of opportunities to spend time alone with your emotions and ideas.

You are happy and at peace with your life, and this makes you feel pleased.

The sound you are hearing is that of a soft wind rustling the leaves as it passes through the area. You go out into a path that is lighted only by the moon, and the earth under your feet is pleasantly cold.

You have a sense of satisfaction, calm, and ease with the way your life is going.

You have an attitude of gratitude for the mundane but meaningful aspects of your existence.

You are free to meditate for as many minutes or hours as you see fit.

When you are ready, slowly open your eyes and greet the new day with a cheerful expression on your face.

Meditation for the Relaxation of the Body

Locate a nice, quiet spot where you may sit comfortably and find a space there. Turn down the volume on the phone, and dim the lights. This is your opportunity to experience inner serenity and tranquility, and you may do so by relaxing and unwinding at this time.

Put your hands on your lap and check to see whether you have enough warm clothing on. To begin, you should shut your eyes in a relaxed manner.

Inhale slowly and deeply, then hold that breath for a few seconds. Feel a little pressure on your chest, and let the air out of your lungs as slowly as you can.

Once again, inhale slowly and deeply, and then hold that breath for a few seconds. Slowly let the air out of your body.

Take a deep breath in and then out. Take a deep breath in and then out. Take a deep breath in and then out.

Relax and let each breath to carry all of your anxiety and worry away with it. Give your body permission to feel peaceful, and allow yourself to relax even more.

Take a deep breath in and then out. Take a deep breath in and then out. Take a deep breath in and then out.

You are now calm and at ease with both yourself and the people and environment around you.

As ideas that are calming come to your mind, slowly and softly breathe in and out.

Imagine that sense of calm permeating your whole body, starting from your brain and working its way down to every part of you.

Your forehead, temples, and face muscles should feel much more relaxed now.

Relax your jaws and cheeks, and gently let go of any tension you feel in the muscles that surround them.

Permit the sensation to go down to your neck and to penetrate deeply into the muscles of your body. You should now feel less tension in your shoulders. Take several slow, deep breaths to calm your muscles and relieve any stress or tension that they may be holding.

Give yourself permission to feel it all the way down to your arms. You experience a greater sense of ease in your arms, all the way down to your fingers. Take several slow, deep breaths to calm your muscles and relieve any stress or tension that they may be holding.

Permit the sensation to go to your chest, and then let it travel down to your stomach. Observe how your stomach moves up and down with each breath you take. Take several slow, deep breaths to calm your muscles and relieve any stress or tension that they may be holding.

The emotion should be allowed to flow to your back. As the feeling works its way up your spine, you should start to experience a sense of calm and relaxation. Take several slow, deep breaths to calm your muscles and relieve any stress or tension that they may be holding.

Give succumb to the sensation as it travels down your thighs and buttocks. Your thigh muscles, both behind and in front, are beginning to loosen up, and as a result, you should feel more relaxed overall. Take several slow, deep breaths to calm your muscles and relieve any stress or tension that they may be holding.

Permit the sensation to go down to your knees, then your calves, then your ankles, and finally your feet. Every inhale and exhale brings a sense of peace and relaxation to your whole body. Take several slow, deep breaths to calm your muscles and relieve any stress or tension that they may be holding.

Continue meditating for a few more minutes, focusing your attention on your breath as you try to maintain a peaceful state of mind. Take some time to savor this sense of calm and serenity inside you.

Give your thoughts permission to meander in this timeless and expansive setting as you rest. In the event that you become aware of any distracting ideas, you should just still your mind and concentrate on your breathing.

When you are ready to return to your waking state, slowly open your eyes and look about.

10th Place: The Screams of the Unborn

In many families, unwanted pregnancies and abortions have occurred in the past and continue to do so now. On the other hand, in today's contemporary times, our viewpoint has shifted in the way that we look at abortions and miscarriages. We are of the opinion that those who are not born do not deserve a position in either the system or the family. They are brought up rather seldom. They are often analogous to the secrets or concealed facets of our life, which we don't even want to examine ourselves. It's possible that there is still some leeway when it comes to miscarriages, but not when it comes to abortions. Both the mother and the father experience the grief of losing their child when a pregnancy ends in a miscarriage, and they often wonder what caused it. Sometimes it takes the parents a very long time to recover from the loss of their kid after they have been through the anguish. In situations like these, when there is a full awareness of their loss, and when all of the feelings of sorrow and sadness are processed, then it does not have an influence on the system, and even the parents will be able to sooner or later emerge out of the mourning and go for another kid. But despite this, there must never stop being a spot in their hearts reserved for this kid.

Although there are a number of scientific explanations for why miscarriages occur, from a societal point of view, it may be said that these children are willingly giving up their lives for the sake of their parents or to achieve some type of equilibrium at the societal level. Nevertheless, it is necessary to pay respect to them and be aware of their existence. These children yet to be born are considered part of the system in the same way that those who are already born are. They, too, have a place in the system that is distinct and individual to them.

These unborn children are waiting for acknowledgement from their parents, and the parents need to make sure that they do this in the right way, grieve their loss, and offer these children a home in their hearts so that these children may finally rest in peace. It is imperative that whenever the parents speak about their children, they keep these unborn children in their hearts as well. This should happen whenever they talk about any of their children. These children, just like everyone else, have a place for themselves within the context of the family. The future generations get entangled when these youngsters are not given their proper role in the system and especially in the hearts of their parents. It is essential for persons who have more than one relationship to recognise the children they have with each of their partners, regardless of how many partners they have. Even though these were previous relationships, the importance of the children that were born as a result of those relationships cannot be overstated. If these children are not recognised and given their proper place in the system, it is probable that their parents will continue to be entangled with one another. They could move on or have gone on into other relationships, but a part of them is still stuck or linked with their ex-partner, even if they have moved on.

It is not enough for the parents of the unborn children to just recognize the existence of this kid; they must also acknowledge the anguish and distress that this child has endured. It is often seen that once a couple has gone through the process of having an abortion, the tie between them diminishes, and one of the reasons for this is the non-acknowledgment of the anguish that this kid through and the life that he sacrificed in order to maintain this relationship. This load proves to be physically and emotionally taxing for the couple, and as a consequence, either they decide to part ways or their relationship becomes more distant despite the fact that they continue to live together. When a woman decides to have an abortion, there is a chance that she may have the overwhelming feeling that she has been responsible for the death of her own child, whom she adores. Other feelings that may be engaged in this scenario include embarrassment, guilt, the social stigma, or possibly the unrecognized sadness that may be internally pressuring the parents. These are just some of the potential outcomes of this scenario. Therefore, giving appropriate recognition is required.

Children who survive abortions or miscarriages often have the impression that they were never meant to be here on earth. For instance, if a woman had an abortion before giving birth to a son, and the boy is then referred to as the oldest kid, the son may not have the same feelings associated with being the oldest child. It's possible that he doesn't see being the oldest as a position that belongs to him. In circumstances such as these, however, it is the parents who have the responsibility of resolving the unresolved pain. In circumstances involving abortion, one of the most essential things to keep in mind is that both of the parents need to jointly accept responsibility for their actions, fully mourn and grieve over the loss of the child, and also love the child by reserving a space in their hearts for them for the rest of their lives. When there are unresolved and unprocessed emotions, an abortion may develop into an entanglement, which has the potential to become a pattern that is passed down through generations until it is addressed. Abortion, from another point of view, may be seen as a rejection of both oneself and one's spouse, as well as a collective rejection of one's relationship and love. Because of this, it leaves permanent marks on the couple's connection to one another. It is far more difficult for the couple to form an emotional connection when unsolved abortions continue to be a dominant factor in the relationship. This is because of the load of entangled feelings with the kid.

Abortions are neither morally good nor bad under any circumstance. It is the effect that this behavior has, energetically speaking, on the relationship as well as on the family system as a whole in the broader context. Abortions have an influence on society because, when the parents don't accept responsibility for their acts, they are, in effect, removing this kid from their lives. The natural law that governs the structure of the family asserts that there is a place for each and every individual inside the system, and it does not exclude anybody. Therefore, even a kid who was terminated by abortion is a part of the system and has his or her own position in it. Sadness, sorrow, and any other emotions that are experienced by the parents and well processed will guarantee the emotional well-being of the system, but emotions that are repressed or not properly processed will be passed on to the descendants epigenetically. Abortions are kept a secret sometimes, or even most of the time; they are the dark secrets of the family, which cause energy imbalance in the system. The couple could not be aware of the abrupt gap that has developed between them, or they might not comprehend the reason why they are unable to see love reflected in the eyes of one another. The anguish of having to say goodbye to the kid is enough to stop the natural flow of love that exists inside them.

At the moment that they conceive, a woman instantly transforms into a mother, and a man instantly transforms into a father. Therefore, when the kid is lost as a result of an abortion or a miscarriage, the woman is depriving herself of her own flesh and blood. Their responsibilities as parents begin the moment they realize they are capable of having a child of their own. They have become parents regardless of whether or not there is a kid in their physical lives. In situations involving rape or sexual abuse, the absence of the biological father of the victim creates an extremely intricate energy entanglement. This is due to the fact that the emotions involved are quite complicated. In these kinds of situations, the mother will not consent to the father's participation in the system. In the vast majority of cases, the father is not aware of either the pregnancy or the decision to terminate it. This is the point at which a complicated web of interconnections is formed, including the imprint of the mother's abuse, various energy imbalances within the system, and the lack of understanding or lack of responsibility on the part of the father about the pregnancy. When something like this happens, it's possible that both the guy and the woman involved may have to deal with future repercussions in their relationships and with their children. After one or two generations have passed, there will be children who have the impression that something is missing from their environment. Entanglements go unnoticed for a considerable amount of time in circumstances like these because of the intricate connection that exists between the victim and the offender. In point of fact, the entanglement may become much more severe in some circumstances, such as when the act of rape is covered up and the victim does not admit that she was victimized.

Before having an abortion performed on a kid, it is best practice to go through with a few basic rites beforehand, regardless of the circumstances surrounding the connection between the parties involved. This rite may be performed even after a miscarriage or for any abortions that have been performed in the past.

The memories of this kid are kept close to the hearts of both of the child's parents. They choose a name for the kid with plenty of affection.

- On the inside, show this kid the home where the parents are living, the setting, and anything else about the family that you feel it is important for your child to know, such as whether or not he or she has any siblings and so on.

Now you must come to terms with the fact that the kid is making a tremendous sacrifice for the sake of his or her parents by giving up his or her life.

The last thing you should do is tell the kid, "I love you. You will always have a place in my heart. I acknowledge the heavy price you have paid by giving up your life."

The previous clause is really crucial to the overall meaning. There was a life that was aborted or lost via a miscarriage, and this is a fact that cannot be changed regardless of the circumstances. Recognizing this fact is thus very necessary. There is a possibility that we may get the impression that an unborn kid will not experience these feelings and thoughts. However, the reality is that every creature born into the system or yet to be born has the right to join, and along with this right comes a set of experiences and emotions associated with that membership. During this activity, both parents need to be entirely present in the moment together, honest about how they are feeling, and finally, execute the steps with all of the guilt that they have been harboring inside of them.

The load of guilt that parents are bearing may be alleviated by engaging in this deep movement of the spirit while maintaining an attitude of total honesty. They are free to continue moving on with grace in life regardless of whether or not they are still in the same relationship. Couples who are already involved in a romantic partnership will have the ability to see one another in a fresh manner, as if they were beginning a new partnership. And for the couples who have transitioned into a new relationship, they will be able to move on with grace.

A Method That Doesn't Involve Meditating To Witness Your Thoughts

But what if you don't make meditation a regular part of your life? Is it still possible to take a step back and act as a witness to the ideas running through your head? If so, how exactly? Listed below are some ideas to consider:

1. Recognize that the concept is there in your mind.

When a thought that is upsetting or somewhat heated comes into your mind, it is important to acknowledge its existence. Always keep in mind that fighting to put an end to it is pointless since it won't work. You can fight the existence of the idea by simply admitting it. This serves as a reminder that you are only watching it and not giving it any force of your own. After that, let your mind wander to the next idea, and proceed in the same manner as before.

A helpful hint is that this could seem to be irrelevant or inconsequential to you, especially if you have a long list of items that need to be done. However, you should make an effort to acknowledge the existence of the notion in order to reduce the influence it has over you. Stay calm and go with the flow. You won't believe how easy it is after you try it out for yourself.

2. Remain motionless and do not take any immediate actions.

Remain despite this, and do nothing at this time that may be considered an action that is driven by employing the concept. Be conscious of the fact that there will always be enough time to deal with what has to be completed as soon as your mind is clear and free of distractions — after you have expressed all of the distracting and contradictory ideas and gone on. This is something you should keep in mind at all times.

Action-oriented people often have a tough time sitting still and doing nothing. Here's a tip to help. Put an end to the nagging thoughts running through your head that tell you time is passing too slowly. You are wrong. Continue to be there regardless of how uncomfortable it may make you feel.

This is a component of the approach of training oneself to become conscious of one's own thoughts.

3. Allow stillness to envelop you completely.

Permit the stillness that is inside you to fill you up. Take note of the serenity and tranquillity that pervades the atmosphere. This makes it possible for your higher concentration to go through everything and find the answers you're looking for.

Do not feel as if you have failed or that you can't possibly obtain calm and tranquility if you find that it is difficult for you to allow stillness surround you while you are trying to do so. Take a few slow, deep breaths and capture a location that is really calm and peaceful. Imagine being there, completely submerged in the activity you're participating in. The only thing that should be left once all the commotion and stimulation from the outside world has faded away is stillness. Be present with the void and take it into account.

4. Come back into the here and now in a measured manner.

After giving yourself some time to observe your thoughts, make it a habit to bring your attention back to the here and now. You have some say in the direction your journey is going, and you are able to craft solutions that are doable. This is because your cognition is distinct, unclouded, and devoid of notions that are in opposition to one another. You have contributed to making your mental capacity greater.

A helpful piece of advice is to make it a habit to use this strategy whenever you feel the need to realign with your center or discover a haven among the cacophony of everyday life. If you put these methods into practice, you'll find that you're better able to uncover solutions that are cut and dry to the issues you're facing.

www.ingramcontent.com/pod-product-compliance
Lightning Source LLC
Chambersburg PA
CBHW050249120526
44590CB00016B/2272